EUROPA ✦ MILITARIA

THE GUARDS

BRITAIN'S HOUSEHOLD DIVISION

SIMON DUNSTAN

Windrow & Greene

© Simon Dunstan 1995

Designed by Frank Ainscough
Printed in Hong Kong

This edition published
in Great Britain 1996 by
Windrow & Greene Ltd.
5 Gerrard Street
London W1V 7LJ

A CIP catalogue record for this book
is available from the British Library.

ISBN 1 85915 062 4

Dedication: To Ysobel

Acknowledgements:
Many books have been written about the Guards and their
illustrious history; this volume is but a snapshot, both literally
and figuratively, in that long military tradition. Unless
otherwise stated, all the photographs were taken by Simon
Dunstan during the summer of 1995. They depict many of the
diverse tasks undertaken by The Household Division,
culminating in Trooping the Colour, a military spectacle
unsurpassed in the world which is held annually in honour of
the Sovereign's Birthday. None of these images would have
been possible without the kind permission of the Major General
Commanding The Household Division, and the assistance
given to me by Guardsmen of every rank; all received me with
interest and good humour. Be it at the dining table of the
splendid Officers' Mess at The Household Cavalry Mounted
Regiment or sharing a beefburger in the back of a jolting
Warrior, the hospitality extended to me has been of the highest
order. To every one of them I express my thanks, as I do to the
Commanding Officers, Adjutants and Sergeant Majors of each
of the seven Regiments of the Division. However, there are
among them those who must be named for their particular help
and attention:Sergeant Gordon Allison SG; Captain Barney
Branston WG;WO1 (RSM) Martin Brennan IG; WO1 (RSM)
Andy Crawford SG;Lieutenant Colonel Julian Crowe SG;
Lieutenant Martin David Gren Gds; WO2 Brian Elliot WG;
Colonel T M Fitzalan-Howard SG;Lieutenant the Hon.James
Geddes Gren Gds; Captain Piers German LG; Captain Simon
Gill Coldm Gds; WO1 (RCM) Jeffrey Holbrook LG; Major
Michael Hutchings Gren Gds; Sergeant Terry Jones WG;Major
Douggie McGregor RHG/D; LCoH Simon Mackay RHG/D;
Second Lieutenant Paula Nicolas AGC, SG; Captain Simon
Rhodes-Stampa LG; Guardsman Marcus Stephens Gren Gds;
WO2 Mark Thompson Gren Gds; Major Mark Van Der Lande
LG. In addition I wish to thank Captain David Horn MISM, the
Curator of The Guards Museum and a fount of knowledge on
all matters pertaining to The Guards; and also the Public
Information Department of London District including Colonel
(Retd) Jonathan Trelawny OBE, Sergeant Ian Liptrot Gren Gds,
and WO2 A J Warham AGC (SPS).
Lastly, my thanks to Will Fowler, who stepped into the breach
at short notice to assist in the preparation of the text.

The Household Division

...dition does not mean that the living are dead; it means that ... dead are living. (Harold Macmillan, 1st Earl of Stockton; ...me Minister 1957-1963; Grenadier Guards 1914-1918)

One of the most enduring memories for visitors to London is the spectacle of the glittering cuirasses and helmets of The Household Cavalry or the scarlet tunics and black ...rskin caps of the Foot Guards, usually glimpsed during the ...ly ceremonial of the Changing of the Guard. The stirring ...nd of an approaching band followed by the steady crunch of ...el-shod boots, or the clatter of hooves and jingle of harness, ...ailingly turn heads and draw expectant crowds whenever they ...heard.

However, for every Guardsman or Trooper mounting guard ...Buckingham Palace or Horse Guards there are two others on ...rational duties around the world - be it in Military Aid to the ...il Power in Northern Ireland; fulfilling Britain's contribution ...the NATO presence in Germany; or escorting humanitarian ...convoys with the United Nations Protection Force in Bosnia. ... multaneously, The Guards conduct training across the globe in ...diness to meet all manner of threats in every type of terrain or ...ditions, from the frozen wastes of Norway to the arid deserts ...Oman, and from the jungles of Belize to the prairies of ...nada.

The Household Division of the British Army consists of ...e Life Guards and The Blues and Royals, united as The ...usehold Cavalry; and the five Regiments of Foot Guards - ...enadier Guards, Coldstream Guards, Scots Guards, Irish ...ards and Welsh Guards. As Household Troops their primary ...k is to protect the Sovereign and the Royal Palaces and to ...vide escorts and guards of honour on State occasions; but ...like the ceremonial troops of many other countries, The ...ards also represent - as they have done for nearly 350 years - ...professional elite of the nation's fighting army.

An example of this dual identity is provided by the ...ardsmen manning the sentry boxes at Buckingham Palace or ...James's Palace. They are armed with the current British Army ...5A1 5.56mm rifle - a stubby, futuristic-looking weapon with ...ck metal parts and green plastic furniture, which to the casual ...server may seem incongruous in the hands of a soldier dressed ...the scarlet and bearskin recalling a former age of military ...endour. The ceremonial units of some other nations, such as ...rmany and the United States, are issued outdated rifles whose ...gth and centre of gravity make them easier to handle during ...movements of traditional arms drill; and some suggested that ...e Guards should follow this example.

The adoption of the L85A1 recognized the essential ...aracter of The Guards: they are fully operational troops, on ...ty 24 hours a day, 365 days a year to protect the Sovereign. ...vay from the parade ground live ammunition is carried; and ...er last light, The Queen's Guard exchange scarlet and bearskin ...berets and combat fatigues to become "prowlers" around the ...laces and barracks which are their responsibility. The revision ...arms drill to accomodate the short, heavy L85A1 (such as the

Renowned throughout the world, the standard of appearance maintained by the officers and men of The Household Division is of the highest order. In their ceremonial function they are the foremost guardians of an enduring tradition of military splendour and dignity, based upon the foundation of an unsurpassed fighting record stretching back over three centuries. Here the Adjutant of 1st Battalion Grenadier Guards is mounted on a charger displaying State saddlery (only worn in the presence of the Sovereign). This is one of eight sets presented to The Grenadier Guards in 1851 by the 1st Duke of Wellington in his capacity as Colonel of the Regiment.

need to change arms periodically), and the provision of a parade cover for the moving parts to prevent snagging, was a trivial price to pay for maintaining The Guards' capability to move swiftly from a ceremonial to an operational role, carrying for all duties the battlefield weapon with which all ranks are thoroughly trained.

Recent operations

In the past 25 years (or approximately the same period as the 22 years service span of a full-term Guardsman), the troops of The Household Division have spent numerous tours in Northern Ireland, patrolling the streets of Belfast and Londonderry, manning Vehicle Check Points and Observation Posts across the Province, and dominating the "bandit country" of South Armagh. Soldiering in Northern Ireland has been a recurring and constant challenge to all ranks, testing their patience, watchfulness, courage and diplomacy to the utmost.

Over this same period the British Army has been instrumental in deterring the territorial ambitions of Guatemala against the former Central American colony of Belize, and The Guards have played their part in occupying camps and bunkers deep in the stifling, swampy jungle. As part of the United Nations or other multi-national forces, they have patrolled the Green Line in divided Cyprus; have served in Angola, Cambodia/Kampuchea, Rhodesia/Zimbabwe, Sinai, Western Sahara, Northern Iraq, and most recently in the former Yugoslavia - always with restraint and professionalism, in trying and often hazardous situations. In the same period, events in two very distant and different parts of the world have drawn The Guards into full scale hostilities.

The Falklands

In 1982 troops of The Household Division played a significant part in Operation Corporate - the liberation by a British task force of the Falkland Islands in the South Atlantic, occupied by the military regime then in power in Argentina. The Blues and Royals provided 3 and 4 Troops of B Squadron, embarked with 3 Commando Brigade, as a counter to the amphibious tracked landing vehicles and Panhard armoured cars deployed by the Argentinians. Both troops landed with the assault infantry at San Carlos and Port San Carlos, and dug in to await the expected Argentinian counterattack. Each troop comprised two Combat Vehicle Reconnaissance (Tracked) - CVR(T) - Scimitars, armed with 30mm Rarden cannon, and two CVR(T) Scorpions armed with 76mm guns, with a Samson Armoured Recovery Vehicle in support.

When 5 Infantry Brigade, including 2nd Battalion Scots Guards and 1st Battalion Welsh Guards, landed on 1 May, The Blues and Royals were ordered to join the brigade in the area of Fitzroy. The move, expected to take two days because of the atrocious waterlogged terrain, was accomplished in only six hours, demonstrating the remarkable cross-country mobility of CVR(T). On 11/12 June the Scorpions used their 76mm guns in support of the successful night attack on Mount Longdon by 3rd Battalion Parachute Regiment.

On the night of 13 June, 3 Troop supported the attack by 2nd Battalion Parachute Regiment on Wireless Ridge, while 4 Troop provided fire support to the assault by 2nd Battalion Scots Guards on the formidable Mount Tumbledown. The key feature in the Argentinian positions around Port Stanley, Mount Tumbledown was defended by elements of 5th Marine Infantry Battalion. During this hard fought 12-hour battle the Scots Guards lost nine killed and 43 wounded. (In one incident during this action the now-Major Sam Drennan, a former Scots Guards NCO then serving with the Army Air Corps, took it upon himself to fly his Scout helicopter repeatedly into front line positions, under direct enemy fire and during a snow storm, to evacuate 16 wounded Scots Guardsmen.)

1st Battalion Welsh Guards had already suffered heavy casualties when the Landing Ship Logistic (LSL) *Sir Galahad* was attacked by Argentinian A-4 Skyhawk fighter-bombers in Bluff Cove on 8 June. With 350 Welsh Guardsmen aboard, the ship was hit by three 500lb bombs and caught fire; in the ensuing inferno 48 men were killed including 32 Welsh Guardsmen, and a further 60 suffered serious burns. Despite the tragedy the Battalion, reinforced by A and C Companies of 40 Commando Royal Marines, was tasked with the assault on Sapper Hill on 14 June; but the Argentinians collapsed before the attack was completed. The participating Regiments were each awarded the Battle Honour "Falklands 1982".

The Gulf War

Almost ten years later men of The Household Division were in action as part of 1st (UK) Armoured Division in an operation which the British called Operation Granby and the United States, Desert Shield/Sabre. The campaign against Iraqi forces occupying Kuwait saw a squadron of The Life Guards reinforcing the 14th/20th King's Hussars as part of 4 Armoured Brigade. In the short ground action phase the Challenger main battle tanks of The Life Guards, supporting The Royal Scots

Battle Group, made the first contact with the Iraqis on Object Bronze, and subsequently fought a battle with Iraqi tanks Objective Brass. Three squadrons of The Life Guards also ma up the Armoured Delivery Group which, with three armou infantry companies of The Scots Guards, were a reserve of bat casualty reinforcements.

As the most experienced armoured infantry battalion BAOR, 1st Battalion Grenadier Guards sent The Quee Company to 1st Battalion The Royal Scots, and No 2 Compa to 3rd Battalion The Royal Regiment of Fusiliers, both in Armoured Brigade.

The 1st Battalion Coldstream Guards formed part of Prisoner of War Guards Force. This was not the rear a sinecure suggested by that title; the Coldstream were ligh armed "sweepers" following close behind the tanks a armoured infantry on the battlefield, collecting Iraqis a processing them back to Maryhill Camp, the British Po facility. During the operation they handled over 6,000 prisone

For their part in this campaign the Battle Honour "G 1991" was awarded to The Life Guards, Grenadier Guar Coldstream Guards and Scots Guards, and that of "Wadi-A Batin" to The Life Guards and Grenadier Guards.

The Incremental Companies

When the collapse of the Warsaw Pact in the early 199 prompted a government review of British armed forces streng composition and likely deployment ("Options for Change"), three senior Regiments of Foot Guards were each reduced fr two battalions to one. However, they were able to revive traditions of their 2nd Battalions by establishing Incremen Companies, each consisting of 101 men and five officers. Rath than make these Incremental Companies part of their respecti 1st Battalions, where their special identity might be lost, th were deliberately stationed with differently cap-badg battalions. Thus, on 4 August 1994 Nijmegen Compa Grenadier Guards was inaugurated by the Colonel of t Regiment, and is currently attached to 1st Battalion Sco Guards at Victoria Barracks, Windsor. On 31 December 1993 7 Company Coldstream Guards was formed, and curren serves with 1st Battalion Irish Guards at Chelsea Barrack London. In November 1993 F Company Scots Guards w created, and attached to 1st Battalion Grenadier Guards Wellington Barracks, London.

Incremental Companies may originally have been created assist in Public Duties, but they also fulfill a normal operation role and train for war. In 1995 No 7 Company took part in a jo Anglo-Hungarian exercise in Hungary - the first of its kind the British Army; and F Company deployed for two weeks Exercise Cooperative Bridge, a NATO exercise in Poland.

Recruitment and training

As some of their names suggest, the Regiments recruit from t regions of the British Isles. The Grenadier Guards attract recru from the Potteries and Lancashire as well as London and t South-East. Recruits for the Coldstream Guards come from t North and the Scottish borders. Though The Scots Guards attra many men from north of the border, they also have soldiers fro Corby and Blackpool. The Irish Guards recruit men from bo the Catholic and Protestant traditions in Ireland, but also a lar mber from the Irish community in Liverpool. Over 90 per cent The Welsh Guards are recruited from the Principality.

The age of a recruit may be anything between 17 and 25 ars, and many come from families which already have nnections with The Guards. In the past, when a young man s recruited he reported for basic training to The Guards Depot Pirbright in Surrey, where the necessary high standards of n-out and drill were instilled. Following "Options for ange", however, all Regimental and Corps Depots were olished, and five Army Training Regiments were established. ese take recruits through the Common Military Syllabus ecruit), a ten-week programme which covers basic skills cluding physical fitness, drill, weapon handling and rksmanship, fieldcraft, map reading, NBC training and neral military knowledge. This syllabus is mandatory for all ldiers regardless of their future specialization.

The Guards Depot has now become the Army Training giment Pirbright, and trains men and women of the Royal tillery, Army Logistic Corps, and Royal Electrical and chanical Engineers. However, within the ATR, The usehold Division has retained Guards Company, so that ure Guardsmen are trained and instructed by Guards officers d NCOs. The instructors are at pains to ensure that their cruits beat those from the other Corps in all competitions of litary skill and fitness.

Upon completion of his CMS(R) the recruit, now termed a ainee Guardsman, proceeded (until 1995) to the Infantry aining Battalion at Catterick in North Yorkshire to undertake Foot Guards Combat Infantryman Course, for instruction in sic infantry skills and ceremonial drill; to ensure that the cessary high standards of drill are achieved the CIC lasts two eks longer for Guardsmen than for the Line Infantry.

Until 1995 training was carried out by the Guards Training mpany alongside Parachute Regiment Company and Pegasus mpany of The Parachute Regiment; the command element d the manning of HQ Company, Infantry Training Battalion tterick were drawn from Guards and Parachute units. Late in 95 this association was broken, when during further organisation ITB Catterick became Infantry Training Centre tterick; though most of the ITB remained at Helles Barracks, e Guards Training Company moved to Vimy Barracks. The structional staff of the Guards Training Company are still awn from the five Foot Guards Regiments.

There are two main types of commission for officers tering The Guards. The Regular Commission is for those who sh to make the Army a permanent career; subject to a ntinuing review of fitness, competence and requirement, ficers holding the Reg C may hope for a career which will take em to their 55th birthday. A Short Service Commission lasts r a minimum of three years, but can be extended to eight years mutual agreement. The Common Commissioning Course hich trains officers at the Royal Military Academy Sandhurst sts for 42 weeks in three 14-week terms, and there are three tries a year.

There is today no "typical" Guards officer. Many have been lucated at public schools, and many are university graduates; t the old cliché of "Eton, Oxford and The Guards" is just that cliché. Another outworn myth is that all Guards officers enjoy ivate incomes; one serving officer commented, "There are

some - but I can count them on the fingers of one hand". Indeed, many officers now have working wives - which, as throughout the Army, can increase the pressures when battalions are posted away on long tours. As in all good units, shared social and sporting interests and a network of friendships - quite often, kinships - ensure that the battalion is a close knit family; and beyond the battalion, the extended family of The Household Division provides a strong bond across the Regiments and the generations.

Training courses, tests of practical skills and theoretical knowledge, and annual reports all ensure that high standards are maintained by officers, NCOs and men throughout their careers. Maturity, experience and professional knowledge all contribute to the speed at which a man gains promotion. Guards senior non-commissioned officers have a wealth of accumulated practical wisdom, and set the standards and the tone for the soldiers in the battalions.

Guardsmen periodically serve in extra-regimental postings throughout the British Army and in posts abroad. As members of British Army Training Teams men of The Household Division have in recent years taught technical and military skills to soldiers in armies as diverse as those of Mozambique and Georgia.

The Special Air Service and The Household Division have always enjoyed a close relationship since the former's first operations in North Africa under its founding commander, Lieutenant Colonel David Stirling of the Scots Guards. The Guards have supplied officers and troopers, particularly for G Squadron 22 SAS, which was raised in 1966; Guards officers have commanded 22 SAS, notably during the Falklands and Gulf campaigns; and currently two of the four squadron commanders are Guardsmen.

Within the Army at large, Guardsmen currently hold many key positions. These include the Chief of the General Staff, General Sir Charles Guthrie; the Quartermaster General, Lieutenant General the Hon. Sir William Rous, and the Adjutant General, Lieutenant General Sir Michael Rose. At the Royal Military Academy Sandhurst, The Household Division provides the Academy Adjutant, New College Adjutant and one Platoon Commander or Company Instructor as tied posts, together with the Academy Sergeant Major, the Sergeants Major for Old and New Colleges, and no more than 22 or less than 18 of the Colour Sergeants. The unique instructional style and personalities of the specially selected senior NCOs who serve at Sandhurst have remained stamped in the memories of generations of British Army officers.

The British Army, even in today's pared-down numbers, is a remarkable institution - perhaps, in these uncertain times, one of the few institutions which truly retains the confidence of the great majority of the public. At the heart of this institution stand The Guards: a conscious elite, unembarrassed to teach pride in tradition, dedicated to maintaining unsurpassed standards of excellence in performance and presentation. It is an ethos which has stood the test of time, and battle, for some 350 years. Looking around today's world, it is hard to visualise a future in which it will not be needed still.

The Household Cavalry Regimen

S ince the "Options for Change" review the two Regime of Household Cavalry, The Life Guards and The Blues a Royals, have merged to form two composite Regimen The Household Cavalry Regiment and The Household Cava Mounted Regiment.

The Life Guards are the first Regiment in order precedence in the British Army. Originally formed in 1652 as King's Life Guard by King Charles II during his exile Flanders, they escorted him to London following the Restorati of the monarchy in 1660. Reorganised into two Regiments 1788, they were re-amalgamated in 1922. Their fighting reco began in the Low Countries in 1673; before the end of century they also fought at Sedgemoor and The Boyne, and th 18th century Battle Honours include Dettingen and Fonten They fought in the Napoleonic Wars in the Peninsula and Waterloo; and in 1882, as a composite regiment with The Blu under Wolseley during the Khartoum relief expedition.

Throughout the First World War they served on the Weste Front. Converted to the armoured role, The Life Guards foug during the Second World War in the Middle East, North Afri and North-West Europe.

The Blues and Royals were formed in 1969 amalgamation of The Royal Horse Guards (The Blues) and 1st Royal Dragoons. The RHG traced their lineage to a regime

...ised by Oliver Cromwell in 1650; in 1661 they were incorporated into King Charles II's army as The Earl of Oxford's Regiment - "The Oxford Blues", from their uniform colour, which they have retained. Their fighting record closely parallels that of The Life Guards. The 1st Royal Dragoons, raised in 1661 ...s The Tangier Horse and spending their first 20 years fighting the Moors in North Africa, later served throughout the 18th century and Napoleonic campaigns against France, in the Crimea in 1854, in Egypt and South Africa, and in both World Wars.

The Household Cavalry Regiment is the armoured reconnaissance regiment for 3rd (UK) Division. The division has a dual role as part of NATO's Allied Command Europe (ACE) Rapid Reaction Corps and the newly formed UK Joint Rapid Deployment Force, the land element of which is based on 5 Airborne Brigade and 3 Commando Brigade. The Household Cavalry Regiment is based at Combermere Barracks, Windsor.

The Regiment comprises Regimental Headquarters; HQ Squadron; and four Reconnaissance Squadrons - two each found by The Life Guards and The Blues and Royals. Each Squadron has an HQ; three Recce Troops, each with four CVR(T) Scimitars; a Guided Weapons Troop with four Strikers equipped with Swingfire ATGWs; a Support Troop, and a Light Aid Detachment. All sub-units are equipped with variants of the CVR(T) series.

During 1994 the majority of the Regiment deployed to former Yugoslavia, on a six month tour, as part of the British contingent of UNPROFOR. The first to go was B Squadron in August, followed by RHQ and D Squadron in November, and A Squadron in February 1995. Additional vehicles and troopers were provided to each squadron by C Squadron. In many respects Scimitar is an ideal armoured fighting vehicle for this new role. It is compact, and has a combat weight of only 7800kg giving very light ground pressure; this allows its use on narrow, badly surfaced tracks and most bridges, but on good roads its Jaguar engine gives a top speed of 80kph. The 30mm Rarden cannon can fire both high explosive and armour piercing ammunition out to 4000 metres. Thus a Scimitar could escort convoys of UNHCR aid trucks over any route, had firepower and the protection of armour where necessary, but would not damage the few and often primitive roads through the mountains.

On its arrival B Squadron, under command of 2nd Battalion The Royal Anglian Regiment, was based on the outskirts of Gornji Vakuf. When RHQ and D Squadron arrived they took over operations in an area known as the Maglai Finger which divided Serbs, Croats and Muslims. The RHQ was established at Zepce with D Squadron and an infantry company, collectively known as BRITCAVBAT, spread around the area. In summer 1995 A Squadron returned to the UK.

(Above left) Trooper Grosvenor, a Scimitar gunner of B Squadron, keeps watch during a brief halt while on exercise on Salisbury Plain. In order to maintain their identity as Guardsmen during the Gulf War, the cap badge backing ribbon in Guards colours was adopted as a flash on the right upper arm; and it has been retained as the distinctive badge on the combat uniforms of The Guards.

(Above) A Scimitar of B Squadron pulls into a squadron leaguer during an exercise on Salisbury Plain. Armed with the same 30mm Rarden cannon as the Warrior AIFV, and designed for reconnaissance by stealth, the Scimitar is the standard mount of The Household Cavalry Regiment.

7

(Above) The gunner's image intensification night sight of a Scimitar of B Squadron is exchanged by REME personnel prior to a night-firing exercise at Castlemartin ranges in South Wales. The green flag indicates that live ammunition is stowed on the vehicles but all weapons are clear; a red flag is flown when the weapons are loaded. The squadron has three Scimitar troops each of four vehicles, a Guided Weapons Troop of four Strikers, and a Support Troop of five Spartans.

(Right) Lance Corporal Vost enjoys a chat while guarding Bulk Fuel Installation 1 at Lippe on Route Square in Bosnia. Because of its less belligerent appearance the versatile Spartan has proved especially useful during operations in Bosnia, where it is customarily employed as the troop leader's vehicle, also carrying an interpreter, and with medical personnel often in attendance to assist the civil population. (Photo LCoH Simon Mackay RHG/D)

(Opposite above) 30mm Rarden and coaxial MG tracer rounds light up the sky at Castlemartin ranges.

(Inset) Corporal of Horse Wells consults his BATCO during a "radio stag" in the rear of a Sultan command vehicle of B Squadron. His red beret and parachute wings indicate that he has "passed P Company" and is trained to undertake airlanding operations in support of 5 Airborne Brigade. The Squadron Headquarters comprise two Sultans, a Samaritan armoured ambulance, and a Spartan for the Squadron Corporal Major.

(Opposite below) Commanded by Lance Corporal of Horse Fisher, a patrolling Scimitar halts somewhere on Route Triangle during a routine operation. During a typical ten-day cycle, two days are spent patrolling Route Square, and two days Route Triangle; two days at Prozor; on the seventh day vehicles return to Gornji Vakuf for maintenance; the eighth is spent on guard; the ninth, undertaking G5 "hearts and minds" tasks; and the tenth day off duty (with a strict limit of two cans of beer per man...), before the cycle is repeated. (Photo LCoH Simon Mackay RHG/D)

(Left) With the passing of the Cold War the deployment of British soldiers to serve in the blue helmets of the United Nations becomes increasingly commonplace. Here, Lance Corporal of Horse Rogers is typical of Britain's contribution to the UN Protection Force in former Yugoslavia, where the British Army is highly regarded for its professionalism, impartiality, and refusal to partake in the rampant corruption which is prevalent among so many of the factions involved in the conflict. (Photo LCoH Simon Mackay RHG/D)

(**Below**) Running repairs are undertaken on the Troop Corporal of Horse's Scimitar at Fort Redoubt, a Royal Engineers position on Route Triangle through the mountains. Despite their constant use the CVR(T) vehicles in Bosnia have proved to be commendably reliable; mileages of 600 miles per vehicle per month are normal. (Photo LCoH Simon Mackay RHG/D)

(**Above**) A Scimitar of 2 Troop, A Squadron, halts at BFI1 on Route Square. In Bosnia the normal troop complement is three Scimitars and one Spartan, in each of five troops in a squadron; Squadron Headquarters has two Sultan command vehicles and a Samaritan ambulance, and the attached REME Light Aid Detachment one Samson recovery vehicle and two Spartans. Few modifications have been made to CVR(T) in Bosnia beyond extra stowage bins (all of which have to be kept padlocked to prevent pilfering); studded tracks in the winter months; and the fitting of a black-out curtain from a Sultan CV behind the driver of Scimitar to reduce the draught for the turret crew. Note the cavalry guidon on the left hand aerial, and on the right the UN flag below the Household Cavalry Regiment pennant - red over blue indicates the Life Guards (A and B Squadrons), and blue over red The Blues and Royals (C and D Squadrons). (Photo LCoH Simon Mackay RHG/D)

The Household Cavalry Mounted Regiment

The Household Cavalry Mounted Regiment, which consists of The Life Guards and The Blues and Royals Mounted Squadrons and a HQ Squadron, is the ceremonial face of The Household Cavalry. The HCMR is based at Hyde Park Barracks, Knightsbridge, London. Its main duty is to furnish The Queen's Life Guard at Horse Guards, Whitehall every day of the year. In addition the Regiment takes part in the Garter ceremony, State Opening of Parliament, Queen's Birthday Parade and State visits, and provides escorts to the Sovereign on all other State engagements.

When troopers join the Household Cavalry only one in 20 can ride; indeed, those with previous riding experience are often more difficult to train because of ingrained bad habits. After ten weeks' training in the Guards Company of the Army Training Regiment at Pirbright, Surrey, those destined for the HCMR are posted to the Household Cavalry Training Wing at Windsor, where over eight weeks they learn to ride a horse and qualify as a driver/radio operator. There is a further 12 weeks of equitation training before they are ready to appear on parade. If they are going to the Household Cavalry Regiment, they are posted to the Royal Armoured Corps Training Centre at Bovington, Dorset, for gunnery and driver training on Scimitar.

(**Far left**) The New Guard found by The Blues and Royals approaches Horse Guards beneath the Guards Memorial.

(**Left**) Once the Guard has been changed, the dismounting Queen's Life Guard becomes the Old Guard and returns to Hyde Park Barracks. Here, an Old Guard of The Life Guards returns to barracks down the Mall; as the Sovereign's standard is not flying over Buckingham Palace Her Majesty The Queen is not in residence, so this is a Short Guard - 12 men commanded by a Corporal of Horse, and no standard is carried.

(**Above**) For over three centuries the Household Cavalry has provided The Queen's Life Guard at Horse Guards Arch in Whitehall; to this day the archway is deemed to be the official entrance to Buckingham Palace. Here a cloaked Trooper of The Blues and Royals acts as the gate sentry at Horse Guards, now the Headquarters of The Household Division. Cloaks are worn throughout the winter or during bad weather in other seasons.

(**Above right**) The Corporal of The Queen's Life Guard leads the two mounted "boxmen" along the stable passage at Horse Guards to their sentry boxes on Whitehall. The horses have been groomed to perfection, even the hooves being painted and polished; the adjective of highest praise within The Guards is "gleaming".

(**Right**) Framed between a pair of London buses, Trooper Cullen of The Blues and Royals in Mounted Review Order is the centre of attention for admiring tourists. Patience and forbearance are necessary qualities for the boxmen, who hear the same inane questions and comments every time they are on duty. Boxmen are relieved every hour, or every half-hour in extremely cold conditions, while the dismounted gate sentry stands a two-hour spell of duty. To be "in the box" is the most sought-after duty when on guard, and only the best turned-out troopers and chargers receive this coveted post.

13

(Above left) Mounted on a grey, Major General Iain Mackay-Dick, Major General Commanding The Household Division, reviews the HCMR in Hyde Park during his annual inspection. This parade is one of the most spectacular to be conducted in London, but does not feature in any calendar of public events.

(Left) With the Squadron Standard of The Blues and Royals to the fore, the Musical Ride return to barracks after the GOC's annual inspection in Hyde Park. The Musical Ride provides an exciting display of military horsemanship at public events. It consists of 16 troopers; four State trumpeters; four Rough Riders (duty men dressed in 19th century stable dress); and a Drum Horse. Historically, lances have never been carried in battle by either Regiment of The Household Cavalry.

(Above & inset) When in Mounted Review Order the farriers - responsible for the care and shoeing of the horses - carry polished poleaxes. In former times, the poleaxe was used to despatch wounded horses and to amputate the hooves of the dead for identification. The initials of the Regiment and the Regimental number are marked on the front hooves, and Army numbers on the back.

(Right) Colonel Peter Rogers, Lieutenant Colonel Commanding Household Cavalry, oversees a Guard Mount accompanied by the Band of the Life Guards on Horse Guards. The frock coat, with its characteristic mohair braiding and olivets, is worn only by officers holding particular appointments. On the left sleeve is a gold embroidered eagle, worn by all ranks of The Blues and Royals since the amalgamation of 1969; this commemorates the capture of the eagle standard of the French 105th Infantry by the 1st Royal Dragoons at Waterloo.

15

(**Above**) With the Guards Memorial framed between them, the Officers of the New and Old Guards exchange orders, with The Life Guards to the left and The Blues and Royals to the right - the most obvious difference in uniforms being that the former wear scarlet tunics and white helmet plumes, while the latter have blue tunics and red plumes. The full dress uniforms of the Regiments of Household Cavalry have remained virtually unchanged since the Crimean War. Common to both Regiments are the white metal helmets and cuirasses, as well as a white cross belt with a narrow red flask cord; at the back is a black leather box adorned with a brass Royal Coat of Arms, which was formerly used to carry carbine cartridges.

(**Right**) The Officer of the New Guard and the Standard Coverer flank the Standard Bearer with the Squadron Standard of The Life Guards. Swords are always carried drawn when the standard is uncovered (the cover can be seen draped over the white sheepskin saddle cover of the nearer horse).

(**Opposite**) Constantine, the senior Drum Horse of The Life Guards. To carry the weight of the silver kettledrums, at 68lbs (32kg) each, HCMR Drum Horses are specially chosen for their build and temperament, normally being skewbald or piebald geldings; they are a personal gift of Her Majesty. It takes some 18 months to train them - at least twice as long as a troop horse. They are controlled by reins attached to the stirrups.

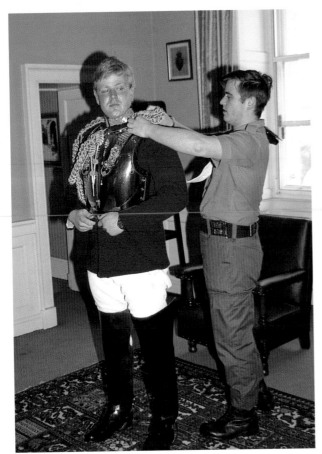

(**Above left**) The Officer of The Queen's Life Guard is prepared by his orderly in the officer's apartment at Horse Guards prior to his return to barracks as the Guard "makes down" following the departure of the Sovereign from London. The two halves of the cuirass are attached together at the shoulder by brass scales.

(**Above**) Lance Corporal Radford mounts his grey in the stableyard at Horse Guards before returning to barracks; Trumpeters and Musicians do not wear cuirasses on parade. Greys have traditionally been the mounts of trumpeters since 1685 on the order of King James II, so that they would be easily distinguishable in battle - in the days of mounted cavalry engagements it was vital for a troop commander to have his trumpeter always close at hand. Trumpeters of The Life Guards wear red helmet plumes, and their horses have black horsehair throat plumes or "beards" with a red core.

(**Opposite below**) Behind the scenes after The Queen's Birthday Parade, a group of officers display a fine selection of the uniforms of the HCMR; from left to right: the Squadron Leader of The Blues and Royals Mounted Squadron; the Riding Master; Lieutenant Colonel Toby Browne, the Commanding Officer, in Dismounted Review Order; the Regimental Veterinary Officer, and the second in command of The Life Guards Mounted Squadron.

(**Above**) The Riding Master, Major Douggie McGregor, in Service Dress Mounted Order, judges the tentpegging competition at the Regiment's annual camp in Norfolk. He holds a position of considerable importance within the Regiment, being responsible for all aspects of horsemanship - the breaking and schooling of remounts; the training of all new recruits; the presentation of the Musical Ride, and all matters of equitation at ceremonial parades and competitions.

Central to the life of the Household Cavalry Mounted Regiment are its horses. Known as Cavalry Blacks, most are bought from Ireland as three- or four-year-olds and stand at least 16 hands. It takes eight to ten months to train a new mount to the standard required by the Riding Master.

Within 20 weeks of joining the Regiment a recruit (now termed a Rider) with no previous riding experience can become a qualified Mounted Dutyman Class 3 capable of performing all ceremonial duties, including that of "boxman", if his turn-out is of the necessary standard.

(**Right**) A young visitor to the annual Regimental Open Day at Bodney Camp sits astride Belisarius as he is led by a Trooper of The Blues and Royals dressed in Service Dress Mounted Order. At 18 hands high and 18 years old, Belisarius is the senior Drum Horse of The Blues and Royals; young Ysobel is an imperceptible load compared to what he normally carries on parade.

19

The Grenadier Guards

The First Regiment of Foot Guards traces its origin back to 1656 when it was formed by Lord Wentworth for the exiled King Charles II. The Regiment has earned nearly 80 Battle Honours over 300 years, beginning with Tangier in 1680; it fought under Marlborough in the early 18th century, at Dettingen in 1743, and in the Peninsular War from Corunna onwards. It earned its present title, First or Grenadier Regiment of Foot Guards, when it broke the final French attacks at Waterloo on 18 June 1815; at the climax of the battle the 2nd and 3rd Battalions, rising from prone positions in the corn at the personal order of the Duke of Wellington, fired devastating volleys into the massed ranks of Napoleon's bearskin-capped Imperial Guard. Soon after the battle HRH The Prince Regent approved the adoption of a version of the bearskin. The Grenadier Guards are the only Regiment in the British Army to have gained their title as the result of an action in battle. The Grenadiers distinguished themselves in the Crimean War, winning four of the very first Victoria Crosses awarded (the first of 13 awarded to date); they fought under Kitchener at Omdurman in 1898, and in the Boer War.

Four battalions fought in France in 1914-18, when 34 Battle Honours and seven Victoria Crosses were awarded. During the Second World War three battalions fought with the British Expeditionary Force in 1940; and three more were subsequently

(**Right**) Within the Foot Guards there remains a specific height requirement for Guardsmen in The Queen's Company of 1st Battalion Grenadier Guards and The Prince of Wales's Company of 1st Battalion Welsh Guards; the recruit must be six foot or over in his stockinged feet, calibrated against a measuring stick. (The tallest man in the Household Division at the time of writing was Guardsman Ruddick of the Coldstream, at seven feet.) In the Grenadier Guards, The Queen's Company Sergeant Major is the final adjudicator in such matters. CSM Thompson is wearing Barrack Dress Drill Order with the crimson silk sash denoting Warrant Officer's rank or Battalion Staff. On his right wrist, worn on a strap when in shirtsleeve order, is an additional badge of rank, the crown denoting Warrant Officer 2nd Class. A further indicator of rank is the number and width of the gold lace bands on the peak of his forage cap.

(**Right**) A sight to instil
intimidation in any Guardsman as
he would, the Sergeant Major
1st Battalion Grenadier
Guards, shouts commands to the
parties during the Mounting of
Guard at Wellington
Barracks. Note that the peak of
the forage cap has been "slashed"
so that it becomes almost parallel
with the forehead - an unofficial
modification popular with senior
NCOs in the Foot Guards for its
smarter appearance.

...rmed, the 1st, 2nd and 4th converting to the armoured role and
...hting in North-West Europe with the Guards Armoured
...vision and the 6th Guards Tank Brigade. The 3rd, 5th and 6th
...ttalions fought in the Middle East, North Africa and Italy.

Today's 1st Battalion Grenadier Guards comprises a
...eadquarters Company, with HQ, Quartermaster staff, Signals
...atoon, Motor Transport Platoon, and administrative elements;
...ee Rifle Companies (The Queen's Company, No 2 Company,
...d Inkerman Company); Support Company, with Mortar, Anti-
...nk and Reconnaissance Platoons; and the Corps of Drums,
...ich on active service becomes the Machine Gun Platoon
...thin Support Company.

Throughout 1995 the 1st Battalion was based at Wellington
...rracks in London undertaking Public Duties, and in 1996 at
...llykinler in Northern Ireland to begin two years on a
...sidential tour of duty. The training for their role in Northern
...eland was similar to that undertaken by all battalions serving in
...e Province before the 1994 ceasefire, but with a greater
...mphasis on community relations.

(**Left**) The famous bearskin cap
now worn by all Guardsmen was
originally bestowed on the
Grenadier Guards in recognition
of their defeat of Napoleon's
Imperial Guard at Waterloo.
Although it is surprisingly light
due to the wicker frame, visible
here, the headband can become
constricting after a time, leading
to headaches if not correctly
fitted. The men's caps are shaken
out to give a full look, whereas
officers' bearskins are normally
groomed downwards and
backwards. No bears are killed
specifically for The Guards, and
any bearskins required are
obtained following the annual
culls of black bears in Canada
and Russia. At an average cost of
£600, bearskin caps often last for
over a century, fire and moths
being the main hazards they face.
This bearskin belongs to a Full
Sergeant, indicated by the red
sash, who in the Grenadier
Guards is known as a Gold
Sergeant.

(Left) Despite advances in technology, the load of the infantryman on today's battlefield has not significantly diminished over the years. Here The Captain of The Queen's Company, Major Michael Hutchings, casts his eyes over the proceedings during a field exercise. In The Queen's Company the company commander is Her Majesty The Queen; the effective commander, a major, is known as The Captain of The Queen's Company while the second-in-command, who is a captain or a subaltern officer, is known as The Second Captain! As the premier company in the senior Regiment of the Foot Guards, the command of The Queen's Company is one of the most prestigious positions in the Army.

(Right) Street fighting is known in the British Army as FIBUA – Fighting In Built Up Areas. With enemy "orange" forces lying "dead" around the corner, a Guardsman of The Queen's Company prepares to hurl a smoke grenade to mask the advance of his section towards the next strongpoint, while the kneeling Guardsman prepares a thunderflash to "grenade" its defenders. Note the torch taped to the barrel of the rifle leaning against the wall, which allows the user to acquire targets once inside the darkened buildings.

(Right) Major Hutchings is wearing Temperate Combat Uniform and CEFO (Combat Equipment Fighting Order), which is also shown laid out with, from top left: Combat Body Armour, normally worn under the jacket; 90 Pattern Personal Load Carrying Equipment (PLCE) in DPM-finish nylon; radio receiver; and the contents of the pouches, including maps and "battle library", rations, wound dressings, camouflage cream, etc. At bottom are his L85A1 rifle, bayonet, and ammunition in 30-round magazines. The total load is approximately 44lbs (20 kilos) - or the standard baggage allowance on international airlines.

(**Left**) Once the objective has been reached it must be broken into; the enemy are assumed to have booby-trapped or barricaded all points of entry. Under the covering fire of an LSW gunner, a section commander acts as a step-up for his men as they break in through a window. Once they are inside the section must clear the pitch-dark building from cellar to attic; intimate teamwork and close adherence to battle drills are vital to success in this type of fighting.

(Left) One day street fighting, and the next rehearsing for The Queen's Birthday Parade: here The Second Captain, Lieutenant Martin David, inspects The Queen's Company at Wellington Barracks before it marches to Horse Guards. The most obvious differences between an officer's uniform and that of the other ranks is the taller bearskin (11½ins at the front as against 9ins), the wide red trouser stripes, and the gold or crimson waist sash in place of the white belt. Note the "grenade fired proper" badge worn on the uniform collar by all ranks, and the Grenadiers' evenly spaced buttons.

(Below) On the parade ground at Wellington Barracks Drill Sergeant Smith of 1st Battalion Grenadier Guards indicates to the Subaltern and Ensign of No 4 Guard (found by The Queen's Company) the finer points of sword drill in preparation for The Queen's Birthday Parade. The Drill Sergeant is an appointment particular to the Foot Guards; he and the Assistant Drill Sergeants are responsible to the Sergeant Major for all drill and ceremonial matters, as well as assisting him in assigning duties throughout the Battalion.

(Right) The LAW94 is a one-shot disposable anti-tank weapon which is also effective against bunkers and fortifications, with a battlefield range of 500 metres. The target is acquired by means of a 9mm spotting rifle ballistically matched to the rocket-propelled warhead, which is capable of defeating more than 500mm of armour. Weighing almost 10kg, it has to be carried in addition to all other equipment and ammunition. There is a wartime allocation of eight per infantry section.

(Below) The Kenyan bush allows complete battalion exercises with live firing of support weapons and field artillery. The jungle phase includes training in patrolling, counter-ambush techniques and combat survival; here members of the Recce Platoon receive instruction from a member of 22 SAS. They wear No 9 Dress, Tropical Combat Uniform. The Guards have provided many personnel to the Special Air Service since its inception, usually serving with G Squadron. (Photo Guardsman Marcus Stephens GG)

(Above) The standard rifle currently on issue is the 5.56mm Individual Weapon SA80 (L85A1), now known simply as "the rifle". It is a highly accurate weapon aided by its x4 SUSAT sight, giving an effective battlefield range of 300 metres; but criticism has been made of its lack of robustness in the field and the degree of maintenance required to keep it serviceable. Shown to advantage is the GS Mark 6 combat helmet with DPM cloth cover and camouflage garnishing loops.

(Above right) Guardsman Watkinson "bombs up" prior to a platoon attack by The Queen's Company during the Infantry Field Firing Camp at the Sennybridge training area in Wales; while assigned to Public Duties the resident Foot Guards Battalions take every opportunity to escape the capital to practise their military skills in training areas around the country. The LSW (Light Support Weapon) shares an 80 per cent commonality of components with the standard rifle, but has a heavier barrel and a bipod for more controlled automatic fire. There are two LSWs in each infantry section of eight men - one in each of the four-man fire teams.

(Right) The ultimate Close Quarter Battle drill is the use of the bayonet - a skill learnt during the Combat Infantryman's Course at the Infantry Training Centre at Catterick. Here the technique is demonstrated by Sergeant Vacher of The Queen's Company during Exercise Mad Dragon at the Stanford training area near Thetford in Norfolk. The short length of the L85A1 requires the thrust to be made with the right hand on the end of the butt - just as it was when 18th century Guardsmen wielded their "firelocks" against the French.

Uniforms of the Foot Guards

A t a cursory glance the uniforms of the five Regiments of Foot Guards all look alike, but they are distinguishable by three main features of Guard Dress - the spacing of the buttons on the tunics; the insignia on the collars and epaulettes; and the position and colour of the plume in the bearskin. These and other differences are as follows:

Grenadier Guards

Buttons evenly spaced. "Grenade fired proper" on tunic collar. White plume on left of bearskin. Red band on forage cap; cap and beret badge, the grenade.

Coldstream Guards

Buttons spaced in pairs. Star of the Order of the Garter on tunic collar. Red plume on right of bearskin. White band on forage cap; cap and beret badge, the Garter Star.

Scots Guards

Buttons spaced in threes. Thistle on tunic collar. No plume in bearksin. Red, white and blue diced band on forage cap; cap and beret badge, the Star of the Order of the Thistle.

Irish Guards

Buttons spaced in fours. Shamrock on tunic collar. Plume in St Patrick's blue on right of bearskin. Green band on forage cap; cap and beret badge, the Star of the Order of St Patrick.

Welsh Guards

Buttons spaced in fives. Leek on tunic collar. White/green/white plume on left of bearskin. Black band on forage cap; cap and beret badge, the leek.

(**Above**) Standing beside Drum Major Binns in State Dress, the Captain of The Queen's Company shows to perfection the Guard of Honour Order of the Grenadier Guards, with the even spacing of buttons on the breast and cuffs.

(**Left**) No 7 Company of The Coldstream Guards step off from Wellington Barracks, displaying the red plume on the right of the bearskin and the paired spacing of the tunic buttons.

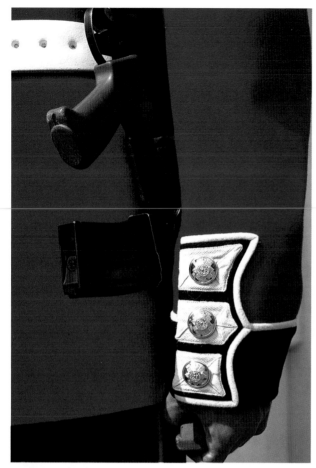

(**Above left**) A Guardsman on sentry duty displays the cuff pattern of The Scots Guards. The design on the button differs in each Regiment.

(**Left**) A Musician of the Band of the Irish Guards is readily identifiable by the blue plume in his bearskin and the shamrock badge on his collar, as well as the Star of St Patrick with the motto *Quis Separabit* on his epaulette. The plume consists of six inches (15cm) of St Patrick's blue cut feathers or bristle, depending on rank.

(**Above**) As the Fifth Regiment of Foot Guards, The Welsh Guards wear the buttons on the tunic breast and cuffs arranged in groups of five. The belt buckle carries the regimental badge and motto, *Cymru am Byth* - Wales for Ever - while the leek motif is repeated on the collar and epaulettes of the scarlet tunic.

(**Opposite top left**) The impressive quality of the Guardsman's ceremonial uniform - here with the specific collar and epaulette insignia and bearskin plume of The Coldstream Guards, and the Bandsmen's and Drummers' shoulder wings - is evident in this portrait.

(**Opposite top right**) Staff Officer of The Household Division in Guard of Honour Order saluting The Queen's Colour of 1st Battalion Grenadier Guards as it leaves Wellington Barracks. The button spacing on the tunic skirts and cuffs identifies an officer of The Coldstream Guards.

The Coldstream Guards

The Coldstream Guards were raised in 1650 as Monck's Regiment of Foot within Cromwell's New Model Army; they take their name from their garrison town on the Scottish border in 1660, when Colonel Monck was instrumental in the Restoration of King Charles II. Their career as Household troops dates from 1661, since when the dozens of Battle Honours awarded to their Colours reflect most of the British Army's most famous campaigns, from Tangier in 1680 to the Gulf in 1991. Thirteen Victoria Crosses have been awarded to members of the Regiment.

Currently based in Germany as an armoured infantry battalion in 4 Armoured Brigade, 1st Battalion Coldstream Guards is equipped with the Warrior armoured infantry fighting vehicle. An armoured infantry battalion consists of Battalion Headquarters; HQ Company, with Signals and Motor Transport Platoons and administrative elements; three Rifle Companies; and Support Company. In the Coldstream the three Rifle Companies are numbered 1 to 3; each has 15 Warriors, and is composed of a headquarters with two Warriors; three numbered Platoons with four vehicles each; and a Light Aid Detachment (LAD) manned by the Royal Electrical and Mechanical Engineers. Support Company consists of the Anti-Tank Platoon with 24 Milan ATGW firing posts; Reconnaissance Platoon, with eight CVR(T) Scimitars; Mortar Platoon, with nine L16 81mm mortars mounted in FV432 armoured tracked carriers; and a REME LAD.

In October 1993 1st Battalion Coldstream Guards were deployed to Bosnia in support of UNPROFOR. Besides escorting convoys and manning OPs, the Battalion played an important part in Lieutenant General Sir Michael Rose's "hearts and minds" campaign in Sarajevo when the Regimental Band, in bearskins and scarlet tunics, played at the Olympic Stadium as a demonstration that some normality had returned to the besieged city. In the autumn of 1994 the Battalion returned to Germany where they are based at Oxford Barracks, Munster. In the summer of 1995 the Battalion honed its armoured infantry skills during large scale manoeuvres at the British Army Training Unit Suffield in Canada. They are destined for Victoria Barracks, Windsor, in 1998.

(Right) The platoon commander's Warrior of 2 Platoon, No 1 Company, 1st Battalion Coldstream Guards returns from a battle run on the Hohne gunnery ranges in northern Germany. The Warrior AIFV (Armoured Infantry Fighting Vehicle) has proved to be highly successful in service, earning the Guardsman's ultimate accolade - "a Gucci piece of kit".

(Below) Guardsmen of 3 Platoon, No 1 Company, deploy from their section vehicles and take up fire positions - behind the line of the Warrior's gun trunnions, so as not to compromise the fire support of the 30mm Rarden cannon. Warrior has a crew of three and carries seven infantrymen in the rear; these have no provision for firing their individual weapons from inside the vehicle. Note, at left centre, the two-man crew of the Platoon Headquarters' single 51mm mortar; like its predecessor, the old 2in. mortar, this fires HE, smoke and illuminating rounds.

(Left) A Guardsman disembarks though the power-operated rear door of a Warrior section vehicle; his rifle has a blank firing attachment on the muzzle. Travelling at speed across country in the back of a Warrior is a noisy, disorientating and tiring experience, due mainly to the vibration being transmitted through the feet. Since an air-conditioning system was not a British Army requirement, the temperature inside the vehicle is a constant 5 degrees F higher than the ambient temperature outside; it can be stiflingly hot in summer and unpleasantly cold in the depths of a German winter. With seven men, their personal weapons and equipment, stores, ammunition and rations for a 48-hour battle, the rear troop compartment offers no room for luxuries and no privacy.

(Below) Once trained, Guardsmen of 19 or 20 years of age may be given the responsibility for the running and maintenance of a £1m-plus Warrior - which speaks volumes for the calibre of the modern soldier. Here, the driver of the Warrior *Sevastopol* from 3 Platoon, No 1 Company accelerates his vehicle to the next location; the vehicles of No 1 Company are named after regimental battle honours.

(**Above left**) Company Sergeant Major Fox of No 1 Company discusses ammunition returns with one of his sergeants after a battalion exercise. The complexity of armoured warfare demands a sophisticated and constant supply of ammunition, fuel, lubricants and stores to maintain machines such as Warrior and their crews in the field.

(**Left**) CSM Plumb of No 3 Company sorts 30mm L12A1 TP-T rounds in clips of three before allocation to crews at gunnery practice; the blue colour identifies these as practice rounds. Warrior is armed with a 30mm L21A1 Rarden cannon and a 7.62mm L94A1 chain gun as coaxial armament, with an effective range of 2000 metres. For servicing duties vehicle crewmen wear a one-piece green denim overall, replaced under battle conditions by a Nomex fire-retardant CVC suit.

(**Above**) Lance Sergeant Hunter in his capacity as Gunnery Instructor, boresights the 30mm Rarden cannon of a Warrior of No 3 Company before gunnery practice on the Hohne ranges; this is the procedure by which the sights are precisely aligned with the main armament for accurate shooting.

(**bove**) Scoff time - men of 3
atoon, No 1 Company, prepare
conburgers over a gas burner
ring a halt between training
ks. In the armoured infantry
e it is rare to find time to cook
ring an exercise; the vehicles
e more often than not moving
the next assignment between
ining serials. The gas cooker is
ersonal item, but this
uardsman is using the lid of the
my issue No 1 petrol burner as
rying pan.

(**Right**) The No 1 of an 81mm
mortar crew adds augmenting
cartridges to a mortar bomb in
the back of an FV432 tracked
carrier prior to a live-firing
exercise on Range 20 at Hohne.
The yellow band around the
bomb indicates High Explosive;
with a full Charge 8 a range of
5,560 metres is possible. Note
the black jerboa insignia of 4
Armoured Brigade beneath the
Guards flash on the right
shoulder.

The Scots Guards

The Scots Guards were raised in 1642 by King Charles disbanded after the Royalist defeat at Worcester in 165 they were reformed in 1660, and moved from the Scotti to the English establishment in 1686. Under various titles th fought in all the British Army's major campaigns, being award more than 90 Battle Honours, from Namur 1695 through t French wars of the 18th century and Napoleonic period, t Crimean War, Egypt, the Boer War, both World Wars, Malay Borneo, Northern Ireland, the Falklands and the Gulf W Eleven Victoria Crosses have been awarded to members of t Regiment.

In June 1994 the 1st Battalion deployed to East Tyrone Northern Ireland on a roulement tour. Roulement tours, whi have been a regular feature in the life of all the infan battalions of the British Army for many years, are six -mon tours unaccompanied by wives or dependents. During such tou the Support Company is often temporarily reduced in order increase the patrol strength of the Rifle Companies - which in Battalion Scots Guards are termed Right Flank, C and Left Fla Companies. A number of successful operations led to the arre of terrorists by the RUC before, in autumn 1994, the ma Republican and Unionist paramilitary groups declared ceasefire which is still holding at the time of writing.

Based in late 1995 at Victoria Barracks, Windsor, 1 Battalion Scots Guards - like all battalions undertaking Pub Duties - are classed as a National Defence battalion and devote 50 per cent of their training time to polishing operational skills. Without leaving London there is considerab scope for classroom work and instruction in first aid, signa nuclear, biological and chemical warfare, vehicle recogniti and vehicle maintenance. The Guards take every opportunity get away from the capital to practise field firing and compa and platoon tactics in training areas such as Salisbury Pla Stanford or Sennybridge. In March 1995 the Battalion was t first unit in the British Army to use the laser-based Tactic Engagement Simulation Equipment in an exercise (TESEX) Salisbury Plain - this is an improved British equivalent of t American MILES equipment. In late summer they took part Pond Jump West, a six-week training exercise in Canada.

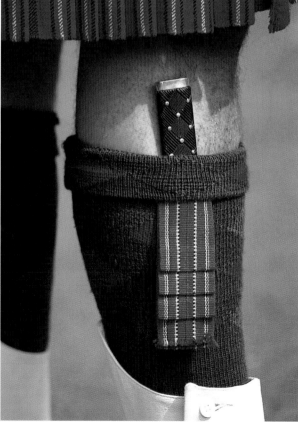

(Above left) The only men in the British Army allowed to wear beards are the Pioneer Sergeants found in some Regiments, whose duties include carpentry, joinery and similar practical work. In his No 2 dress, Lance Sergeant Parkes displays the forage cap of the Scots Guards. The embroidered shoulder title in Regimental colours worn on the khaki Service Dress jacket is particular to the Guards since th demise of the old Battledress in the 1960s.

(Left) Detail from the Pipers' Full Dress uniform, with kilt in Royal Stewart sett, hose, belled garter, dirk, and spat.

(Above left) Two Colour Sergeants show the scarlet tunic and bearskin cap of Guard Order to advantage; note the handsome right arm badge. During The Queen's Birthday Parade of 1995 Colour Sergeant Cameron (left) carried the battalion's cased Colour onto Horse Guards, while CQMS Cockett (right) acted as left guide to the Escort of the Colour.

(Left) Public Duties require the Guardsman to stand motionless for long periods, perhaps in hot sunlight. Tricks to avoid fainting include focussing the eyes on a neutral green colour, and wriggling the toes (without moving the boots...)

(Above) CSM Hood of Left Flank Company offers the benefit of his experience to a young Ensign. Note the variations in detail between the officer's and warrant officer's full dress uniforms. The bearskins of The Scots Guards alone have no plume: when the Regiment paraded or fought in bearskins it always held the centre of the line between The Grenadiers and The Coldstream, so no flank identification was necessary.

(Overleaf, p.36 inset) With even the clouds above him seeming to fall obediently into formation WO1 Crawford, the Regimental Sergeant Major of 1st Battalion Scots Guards - uniformed in Guard Order and forage cap - casts a critical eye over the troops on his parade ground at Victoria Barracks, Windsor, prior to the annual inspection by the Major General Commanding The Household Division. Mr Crawford's medals tell a story of active service in Northern Ireland, the Falklands and the Gulf War, and long service and good conduct.

(Overleaf, p.37 inset) The Sergeant Major's badge of rank, on his right arm, is one of the most prestigious and exclusive insignia in the British Army; it is worn by the five Sergeants Major of the Foot Guards Battalions, the Garrison Sergeant Major of London District, and the Superintending Clerks of the Foot Guards. In the Foot Guards generally the RSM is known simply as "the Sergeant Major"; but in the Scots Guards he is called "Tarra", a nickname whose provenance is lost in the mists of time.

(**Above**) The hallmark of all the Scottish Regiments within the British Army: in The Scots Guards "the Drums", combining the Corps of Drums and the Pipes and Drums, is the senior company, commanded by the Adjutant. With their sporrans swirling the pipers return from Mounting the Guard at Windsor Castle.

(**Left**) Lance Corporal Anderson wears one of the most resplendent Full Dress uniforms of the British Army, with plaid and kilt in Royal Stewart tartan.

(**Opposite above**) The Drum Major of The Scots Guards, in Guard Order, checks the time before leading the Regimental Band and the Pipes and Drums to Windsor Castle for the daily Guard Mounting. Each of the Foot Guards bands comprises a Director of Music and 49 Musicians, identifiable by the shoulder wings on their tunics. By centuries-old tradition, the bandsmen act as medical orderlies when on active service.

(**Right**) The Officer of the Windsor Castle Guard inspects the Duties in Victoria Barracks before the Mounting of the Guard; in attendance is the Sergeant-in-Waiting (duty sergeant) of Left Flank, Lance Sergeant Newton, with the "In-Waiting Book" in which is recorded everything of note during the working day.

(**Far right**) Acting as the Colour Point to mark one of the corners of the parade ground, Colour Sergeant McEwan - one of five brothers within the Regiment - stands with the Commanding Officer's Flag denoting that the latter is on parade. A continuity of family service among both officers and men is still a notable feature of the Guards Regiments.

The Irish Guards

The Irish Guards were formed in 1900 at the person command of Queen Victoria, in recognition of the servi of her Irish Regiments of the Line in the early stages the Boer War, 1899-1902. They first saw action in South Afri as mounted infantry; they went on to fight with distinction both World Wars, winning four VCs in the Great War and two the Second World War. Regimental traditions include t presentation of a shamrock to each Guardsman on St Patric Day, by HM Queen Elizabeth the Queen Mother; and - unique in The Household Division - a regimental mascot, in the form an Irish wolfhound, to lead them on parade.

In December 1995 the Irish Guards resumed Public Duti based at Chelsea Barracks, London, having returned from on their second Northern Ireland tour during which they served the East Tyrone battalion. At this time they are a Nation Defence battalion. Though there are times when public duti make a considerable demand on manpower, with Guards Honour for visiting national leaders as well as Guards Buckingham Palace, St James's Palace and Windsor Castle, t Battalion is also required to produce an operational force f security at London's airports. In late 1996 they will redeplo under command of a National Defence Brigade and will l based in Pirbright, Surrey.

A National Defence battalion consists of the Battali Headquarters; HQ Company, including the Signals Platoon, t Medical Officer with the Regimental Aid Post, Quartermast cooks and Regimental Administrative Office. There are thr Rifle Companies - numbered 1 to 3 in 1st Battalion Guar - each with a war establishment of 120 men. The soldiers may transported by 4-tonne trucks, Saxon wheeled APCs, La Rovers, or Chinook or Puma helicopters. Each company h three platoons each consisting of three sections. Each eight-m section has two LSW light support weapons and various scal of issue of the LAW94 infantry anti-tank weapon; there is single 51mm mortar, mainly used for smoke and illuminatir rounds, in Platoon Headquarters. Support Company includes t Reconnaissance Platoon, Mortar Platoon (9 x 81mm tubes Anti-Tank Platoon (24 x Milan ATGW), and, on active servic the Corps of Drums of a Foot Guards Battalion forms t Machine Gun Platoon.

(Above) The Regimental Sergeant Major of 1st Battalion Irish Guards, WO1 Brennan, gets to know the Battalion's new mascot Cuchulain on the day the Irish wolfhound joined up - with the status and pay of a Guardsman. The Sergeant Major's arm badge, with its lion and unicorn supporters, is known in the Foot Guards as "the fighting dogs".

(Opposite above) Callsign Four Zero Alpha - a multiple commander - supervises the unloading drill of his team from No 1 Company after returning from patrol to the "wriggly tin" of a Permanent Vehicle Check Point base during training for a tour in Northern Ireland. Following the ceasefire in the province, troops now patrol in berets rather than helmets.

(Right) Guardsman Hastie of N 1 Company shows the standard patrol order in Northern Ireland issue DPM (Disruptive Pattern Material) "combats"; chest webbing for ammunition pouches, which makes it easier negotiate the many fences and obstacles encountered on rural patrols; and privately purchased Goretex Danner boots - currentl popular for service in Northern Ireland. The radio earpiece, aerial and characteristic "fist mike" identify him as a fire tear leader.

(**Overleaf, pages 42-45:**) Prior to deployment to Ulster all battalions receive extensive training which is constantly updated by the Northern Ireland Training Wing (NITW). The following sequence of photographs illustrates various aspects associated with the "rural package" of the training programme, at Thetford in Norfolk.

(**Pages 42-43:**)
(**Top left**) Members of an Air Reaction Force check their weapons and equipment as they await a call-out.
(**Top right**) Under the direction of the crewchief crouching behind the door-mounted GPMG, the ARF clamber aboard a Wessex 5 from No.72 Squadron RAF. Berets are not worn - they might be sucked into the helicopter's engines.
(**Bottom left**) Once landed at the dropping-off point, and having dispersed at the double to defensive positions to cover the Wessex's departure, the team consult the map to pick a position for a Vehicle Check Point under the guidance of the attached RUC officer - who will know his "patch" intimately.
(**Bottom right**) While the RUC officer questions the driver of a van the team leader, Lance Sergeant McConnell, scans the road through his x4 sight. If any driver should try to run through the VCP, caltrops would immediately be pulled across the road to puncture the tyres.

(**Pages 44-45:**)
(**Top left**) In a separate scenario, a "terrorist" engages a patrol from a farm building; the GPMG is firing live ball ammunition over the heads of the patrol so that soldiers become familiar with the sound of real rounds passing close by.
(**Top right**) As the team rush forward, a member of the Directing Staff has indicated that the team leader has tripped a booby trap. With Lance Corporal McCool down with "serious abdominal wounds", Guardsman Ferguson takes command and orders the patrol to form a defensive perimeter, scanning the hedgerows through their SUSAT sights for any sign of a follow-up attack, as Guardsman Palmer rips open a first field dressing.
(**Bottom left**) While first aid is applied the new team leader hastily consults the map to determine the exact location for a helicopter extraction.
(**Bottom right**) As soon as the Wessex lands the casualty is bundled inside; as his wounds are serious or even life-threatening, this is termed a "grade A casevac" and everything is done to speed him on his way to hospital.

41

The Welsh Guards

The Welsh Guards are the youngest Regiment of The Household Division, raised on 26 February 1915 by order of HM King George V. The number of Welshmen transferring from other Regiments made it possible for the 1 Battalion to mount Guard at Buckingham Palace three days later on St David's Day. The Welsh Guards first saw action at Loos in September 1915, and fought with the Guards Division on the Western Front for the rest of the Great War. In the Second World War two battalions served with the British Expeditionary Force in France in 1940, and went on to fight in the ranks of the Guards Armoured Division in North-West Europe; they were the first units into Brussels on 3 September 1944, after a hundred-mile advance in one day. A third battalion fought in North Africa and Italy with 8th Army. Reduced after the war to a single battalion. The Welsh Guards have since seen active service in Palestine, Egypt, Aden, Cyprus, Northern Ireland and the Falklands.

In 1994 the Battalion served a residential tour in Northern Ireland where it was based at Shackleton Barracks, Ballykelly; during the last three months it provided security for the rebuilding of the Royal Ulster Constabulary post at Crossmaglen and covered the routes along which convoys ferried men and materials (Operation Rectify). Returning to England, 1 Battalion Welsh Guards are currently based at Clive Barracks, Tern Hill, Shropshire.

(Right) With a red dragon tattooed on his forearm, there is no mistaking the allegiance of Lance Sergeant Pimm of the Regimental Police, manning the gate at Tern Hill Camp. Beneath the Welsh Guards shoulder title he sports the blue macaw insignia of 143 Brigade, a Territorial Army formation for which the Battalion currently provides the Regular element.

After a spell in March-April 1995 as the Spearhead Battalion - an infantry battalion held at readiness to move anywhere in the world at 24 hours' notice, the advance party leaving within two hours - The Welsh Guards are now classed as a Type B Battalion. Their primary role is regional security, and they provide the Regular element of 143 (West Midlands) Brigade, a Territorial Army formation. Between periods of conventional training and exercises in the Welsh Marches the Battalion has sent elements to serve in harsher surroundings. In May 1995 The Prince of Wales's Company (as the senior Rifle Company is entitled) deployed on Operation Chantress, a three-month UN mission in Angola; August saw No 2 Company deployed to Belize for jungle training; and in November Operation Fresco took Guardsmen to Merseyside in Military Aid to the Civil Community, to man 1950s-vintage "Green Goddess" fire engines when the local fire brigade timed a strike to coincide with Guy Fawkes Day.

(Far left) When deployed into the field the Corps of Drums becomes the Machine Gun Platoon of Support Company, equipped with the 7.62mm GPMG (General Purpose Machine Gun) - mounted on a bipod in the light role or on a tripod for the sustained fire role. With nine GPMGs in the platoon, a formidable volume of fire support is available to the Battalion; the 7.62mm calibre has a far greater terminal effect than the 5.56mm of the rifleman. Here the GPMG is on the low mounting, with the No 1 serving the gun, the No 2 feeding the ammunition, and the section commander directing the fire while spotting for targets through his SUSAT sight.

(Left) Drummer Barlow of the MG Platoon prepares to move off for a night exercise in full Marching Order with weapons and ammunition - commonly referred to as "Christmas Tree Order".... The GPMG itself weighs 10.9kg; the spare barrel bag, 12.7kg; the tripod, 13.9kg; each man's Bergen rucksack, 30kg, and his webbing equipment 15kg; while 200 rounds of boxed ammunition weighs 7.7kg. Of all the cruelly burdened infantry the MG Platoon perhaps fare worst, with individual loads of over 100lbs (approximately 50 kilos).

(Above) Dawn - it has been raining for over five hours, and after an arduous approach march through the pitch-black woods everyone is soaked to the skin. Guardsman Gibson and his colleagues of No 3 Company, 1st Battalion Welsh Guards, collect their thoughts at the forming-up point prior to a company attack during Exercise Mad Dragon.

(Left) The attack goes in, and a Guardsman leaps into an enemy position under the covering fire of his comrades of 9 Platoon. The enemy, distinguished by an issue of desert camouflage uniforms, are provided by the Royal Welsh Fusiliers.

48

(Above) During the "reorg" on the objective, prisoners and "enemy dead" are searched for weapons and intelligence material. In a combined two-man drill, one Guardsman leaps onto the back or chest of a prostrate enemy to ensure that he is not feigning death or injury. He is then rolled over, with his body shielding the two searching Guardsmen in case of booby traps hidden beneath it. Meanwhile the second Guardsman covers every movement with his rifle.

(Right) The battered khaki beret of Lance Sergeant Ryan, with its Guards flash and Regimental badge, tells its own story of many weeks in the field; a pristine example is reserved for barracks and public show. As other units of the British Army gradually adopted the khaki beret in place of the dark blue GS type, The Household Division introduced the blue/red/blue badge backing in 1989 to distinguish Guardsmen in the field.

(Left) As Welsh units have so many men named Jones, Williams, Evans, Hughes, *et al*, it is customary in the Battalion to refer to each man by his name plus the last two digits of his Army number - or more commonly, simply by the latter. Here the Regimental Police Sergeant, "Jones (71)", confers with the Picquet Officer outside the Officers' Mess with Lance Corporal Baldwin, displaying the Regimental Police brassard, in attendance. The NCOs wear No 1 Dress or Blues, and "71" carries a picquet cane as a mark of his appointment. The Subaltern wears Service Dress and Sam Browne.

(Above) A stripped-down Serie III 109 Land Rover of the Reconnaissance Platoon, 1st Battalion Welsh Guards, speeds along a forest track during Exercise Mad Dragon. With six Land Rovers, each with a crew four, the primary role of the Recce Platoon is to search out t enemy while advising Battalion Headquarters about his strength, dispositions and likely objective Other tasks include the manning of observation posts; protecting the Battalion flanks or liaising with flanking units; and dealing with enemy heliborne landings rear areas.

(**Above**) Guardsman Pritchard (02) mans the GPMG on a Recce Land Rover; Guardsman Peters looks on, while Guardsman Jewa cradles his L96 7.62mm rifle in his role as a battalion sniper. Wearing their characteristic "ghillie suits", snipers act in pairs, often at the forefront of the battalion to engage priority targets or to oversee likely avenues of enemy approach; they often work in conjunction with the Reconnaissance Platoon. Their marksmanship skills are of necessity outstanding, and head shots at over 500 metres are consistently achieved.

(**Right**) While on exercise, comfort is the order of the day once back in the "admin area" for the evening meal; so Guardsman Hughes (03) replaces his helmet with a woolly hat emblazoned with the Welsh dragon. Of all the Regiments of Foot Guards the Welsh remain truest to their title, around 90 per cent of the men and many officers boasting Welsh parentage or other close connections with the Principality.

51

(Left) The officer commanding 9 Platoon, No 3 Company, 1st Battalion Welsh Guards - Lieutenant Harry Legge-Bourke - takes a welcome swig of water and a smoke after an exhausting house-clearing operation during Exercise Mad Dragon.

(Right) Attired in Mess Kit, the same Subaltern enjoys a glass of wine during a summer function outside the Officers' Mess at Tern Hill. On each lapel is the leek insignia of The Welsh Guards; above the left collar badge is worn a miniature of the Military General Service Medal, with Northern Ireland clasp and the oakleaf of Mentioned in Despatches. The crimson sash indicates that he is the Picquet Officer, essentially the Officer of the Day.

Changing the Guard & The Queen's Birthday Parade

Changing the Guard, which takes place between 11.15am and 12.15pm every day (except during winter months when it takes place every two days) attracts considerable interest from visitors to London. The Queen's Guard detachment at St James's Palace marches to Buckingham Palace where it joins the Buckingham Palace detachment. Meanwhile the New Guard, led by a Regimental Band and Corps of Drums, marches from Wellington Barracks to Buckingham Palace. The Captain of the Queen's Guard symbolically hands over the Palace key to the New Guard, and with it responsibility for the security of the Palace. New sentries are posted and the relieved sentries join what is now the Old Guard. The Old Guard salutes the New Guard's Colour, and the compliment is returned. When the Old Guard has marched off with the band and drums, the New Guard becomes The Queen's Guard. The St James's detachment marches to that palace where the Colour is lodged in the Guardroom.

If Changing the Guard attracts interest, The Queen's Birthday Parade ("Trooping the Colour") provides a spectacle of traditional military glamour, precision drill and martial music second to none in the world.

In historical times a military unit's flag or Colour was the visible rallying point for troops in the blinding powder-smoke and deafening confusion of battle. It was necessary that soldiers should recognise their own flag, and so at the end of each day's march it became the practice to carry them up and down the ranks so that each man could see them; after this ceremony they were hung from a window or over the door of the headquarters. This practical observance became more occasional and more ceremonial as time passed. It is known that The Brigade of Guards carried out a Trooping the Colour parade in 1755; but it was not until 1805 that the custom of Trooping the Colour to honour the Sovereign's Birthday was initiated.

Each year, on the Saturday in June selected as The Queen's official birthday, The Household Division provide eight Guards from the Foot Guards - each of three officers and 70 men - together with the Massed Bands, Drums and Pipes and a Sovereign's Escort of The Household Cavalry Mounted Regiment, for a magnificent parade on Horse Guards in the presence of Her Majesty, in the course of which one of the Colours of the Foot Guards is "trooped". This masterly celebration of traditional military display, the pinnacle of The Household Division's ceremonial calendar, is unfailingly stirring. As the living walls of scarlet and black move in perfect harmony, to the bellowed commands and the crash and blare of the bands, it is also probably the last opportunity anywhere in the world for the observer - through half-closed eyes - to faintly glimpse what an early 19th century army must have looked like when drawn up and manoeuvring for battle.

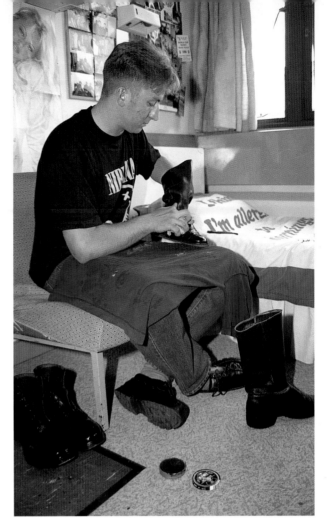

Early on a June morning in 1995 at Wellington Barracks: in his room Guardsman Plant, the orderly to The Captain of The Queen's Company, "bulls" his officer's Wellington boots to the required degree of shine - a task that takes approximately 30 minutes for an experienced Guardsman. The rest of his uniform takes about 60 minutes, with 15 minutes each for his bearskin; tunic; belt and curb chain.

(Left) For a Trooper of The Household Cavalry Mounted Regiment kit preparation takes considerably longer, with the diligent application of Brasso o Autosol to the helmet, cuirass and sword scabbard, black poli to the boots and horse harness, and "Whitesap" to the buckskir gauntlets and horse accoutrements, including the brow band - that essential item for an exemplary turnout.

(Right) The Band of the Irish Guards receives instructions from the Director of Music before dispersing for breakfast - failure to eat breakfast prior to a parade constitutes an offence, because it increases the risk of fainting. Fundamental to The Queen's Birthday Parade is the martial music of the Massed Bands of the Foot Guards together with those of The Household Cavalry.

(Right) The Pipers' black feather bonnets with their distinctive plumes are shown to advantage as Piper "Basher" McCrae lays his pipes, adorned with the company banner of Right Flank, on the bonnet of a Land Rover. Both the Scots and Irish Guards have Pipes and Drums while the other Foot Guards Regiments each have a Corps of Drums.

(Left) All conversation stops as the Pipers of The Scots Guards tune up in the Inner Square at Wellington Barracks. In the background Land Rovers from each of the participating Regiments carry "kits and capes" in case of foul weather.

(Right) The Second Captain, Lieutenant Martin David, and senior NCOs of The Queen's Company, 1st Battalion Grenadier Guards, take the customary medicinal glass of port to lubricate the vocal cords before the parade, so that orders can be more readily heard.

(Below) The Regimental Sergeant Major of the Battalion finding the Escort, WO1 Crawford of The Scots Guards, gives a final briefing to the Right Markers of the Foot Guards prior to stepping off for Horse Guards.

(Above) With Drum Major Binns to the fore, the Regimental Band of the Grenadier Guards leads Nos 3 and 4 Guards out of Wellington Barracks, No 3 Guard being found by F Company Scots Guards and No 4 by The Queen's Company, 1st Battalion Grenadier Guards.

(Left) The Corps of Drums of 1st Battalion Grenadier Guards follows the Regimental Band at the head of Nos 3 and 4 Guards. The drummers wear their distinctive tunics with blue and white shoulder wings, lavishly embroidered with drummer's lace - a *fleur-de-lis* pattern worn since Stuart times to emphasise England's ancient claim to the French throne.

57

(Left) No 6 Guard, found by No 7 Company Coldstream Guards, steps off from Wellington Barracks, followed by No 5 Guard found by Nijmegen Company Grenadier Guards, while F Company Scots Guards took on. This was the first occasion when all three Incremental Companies have appeared on The Queen's Birthday Parade.

(Below left) The Regimental Adjutants of all five Foot Guards regiments prepare to follow the Colour on horseback, while (at right) Lieutenant General the Hon. Sir William Rous, Colonel Coldstream Guards, is being attended by a Lance-Sergeant Groom of the Coldstream. Given its origins in Cromwell's New Model Army, the Coldstream Guards is currently the only Regiment in the Household Division not to have a member of the Royal Family as Colonel. General Rous's great-grandfather fought at Waterloo.

(Right) Colour Sergeant Cameron steps off with the encased Queen's Colour of 1st Battalion Scots Guards between the Escort and No 2 Guard, this being the Colour to be Trooped. Once on Horse Guards it will be uncased and passed to the youngest Ensign in the Battalion.

(Below) The Massed Bands of the Household Cavalry Mounted Regiment form up beneath Buckingham Palace with the Drum Horses to the fore. The kettle drums of The Blues and Royals mounted on Belisarius (foreground) are less ornate than those of The Life Guards on Constantine; but each pair of drums is valued at £1 million, although they are irreplaceable. The Massed Bands number one Director of Music, two Drum Horses and 56 Musicians. This State Dress is worn only in the presence of the Sovereign and on a few other occasions such as the Lord Mayor of London's procession. The richly gold-laced tunic, with the Royal Cypher on breast and back, is worn with a dark blue "jockey cap" similar to that worn by Drum Majors of Foot Guards.

(Left) Horse Guards, during The Queen's Birthday Parade - the supreme annual moment of British military pageantry. (Photo courtesy The Household Division)

(Opposite below) Once the parade is over The Queen returns to Buckingham Palace at the head of her Guards. Here, The Queen's Company of 1st Battalion Grenadier Guards swing down the Mall before marching past The Queen, their Company Commander, and returning to barracks.

(Below) The final act for The Household Cavalry Mounted Regiment is the impressive Regimental Dismount. Irrespective of age or rank, the man on the right of the line gives the signal and the whole regiment dismounts in unison.

(Left) Having flanked Her Majesty The Queen on the saluting dais throughout the parade, Major General Lord Michael Fitzalan Howard, Colonel The Life Guards (left), and General Sir Desmond Fitzpatrick, Colonel The Blues and Royals, arrive at the Officers' Mess in Hyde Park Barracks for lunch. The court appointment of Gold Stick in Waiting alternates between the two Colonels on a monthly basis.

(Right) Once a Guardsman, always a Guardsman, and this fact is reflected in the strength of the Guards Association which has branches across the country and indeed the world. Every year each Regiment holds its own Remembrance Sunday, which includes a brief ceremony at the Guards Memorial and a service in the Guards Chapel. Here a lone piper plays the lament as regimental veterans and the Band of the Scots Guards with the Pipes and Drums in attendance pay their respects at the Guards Memorial in St James's Park facing Horse Guards.

(Below) Under the direction of the Adjutant, Captain Harry Fullerton, the officers of The Household Cavalry Mounted Regiment are marshalled into position for a commemorative photograph to mark the occasion of The Queen's Birthday Parade.

Remembrance Sunday

(Left) A poignant reminder of the passing of battalions, not on the battlefield but by administrative fiat, as veterans congregate for a service of remembrance in the Guards Chapel. It is fervently to be hoped that no more Guards battalions will be lost.

(Above) A veteran of the Grenadier Guards proudly displays his medals during the parade on Black Sunday before he and his comrades retire to the Officers' and NCOs' Messes to mark the occasion in the appropriate manner.

(**Left**) "Endex - show clear!"

(**Back cover**) The Pipe Major, a Drummer and a Piper of 1st Battalion Scots Guards.

The EUROPA-MILITARIA SERIES

Full colour photographic paperback reference books on the armies of today and yesterday, for collectors, modellers, war-gamers, re-enactors, illustrators, and military history students of all kinds.
All 64 pages, 260mm x 190mm,
UK price £10.95, US price $15.95

EUROPA-MILITARIA SPECIALS

All 96 pages, 260mm x 190mm,
UK price £12.95, US price $19.95.

In case of difficulty contact The Sales Manager,

Windrow & Greene Ltd., 5 Gerrard Street, London W1V 7LJ, UK

telephone 0171-287-4570, fax 0171-494-0583